CAT'S OUT OF THE BAG!

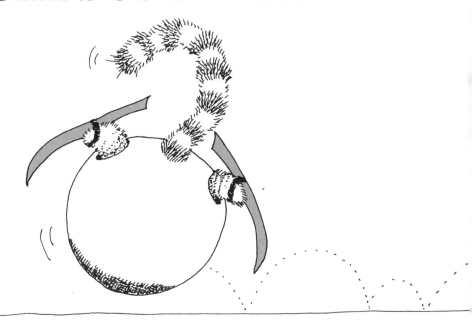

Make Me Laugh!

CAT'S OUT OF THE BAG!

jokes about cats

by Sharon Friedman & Irene Shere
pictures by Joan Hanson

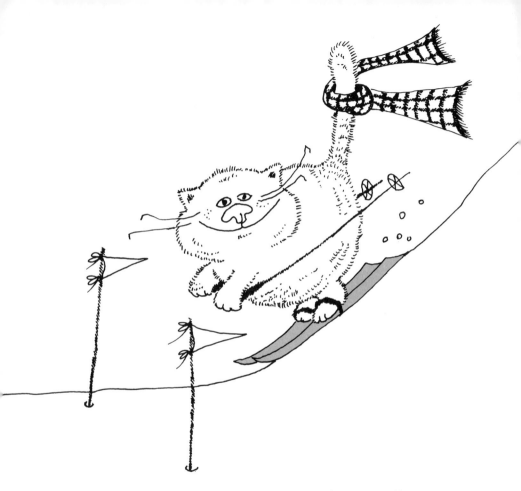

Lerner Publications Company · Minneapolis

To Stephen, Lee, and Robert, whose varied styles of humor have helped promote my own! I love you very much —S.E.F.

To Steve, Holly, and Brett, whose enthusiastic support and love are the true inspirations of my life —I.H.S.

This book is available in two editions:
Library binding by Lerner Publications Company
Soft cover by First Avenue Editions
241 First Avenue North
Minneapolis, Minnesota 55401

Library of Congress Cataloging-in-Publication Data

Friedman, Sharon, 1948-
   Cat's out of the bag!

   (Make me laugh!)
   Summary: A collection of jokes about cats, including
"What do you call a cat that hangs out at the bowling
lanes? An alley cat."
   1. Riddles, Juvenile. 2. Cats—Juvenile humor.
3. Puns and punning. [1. Riddles. 2. Cats—Wit and
humor. 3. Puns and punning] I. Shere, Irene.
II. Hanson, Joan, ill. III. Title. IV. Series.
PN6371.5.F753   1986   818'.5402   85-23858
ISBN 0-8225-0986-5 (lib. bdg.)
ISBN 0-8225-9527-3 (pbk.)

Manufactured in the United States of America

  3   4   5   6   7   8   9   10   94   93   92   91   90   89   88

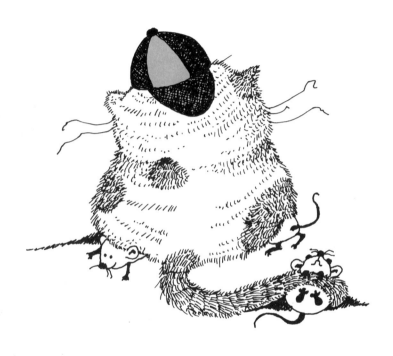

Q: What sport does a cat play with mice?
A: Squash.

Q: Where did the kittens go on their field trip?

A: The mew-seum.

Q: Why did the schoolcat get sent to the principal's office?

A: Because she was a cheetah (cheater).

Q: What did the cat teacher say to his silent student?

A: Cat got your tongue?

Q: What do cats read to their kittens?
A: Cat tales (cattails).

Q: What's a cat's favorite jewel?
A: Purr-ls (pearls).

Q: What do you call a forgetful cat?
A: S-cat-terbrained.

Q: Why did the boy cat like the girl cat?
A: She was purr-fectly a-mew-sing.

Q: What's a cat's favorite color?
A: Purr-ple.

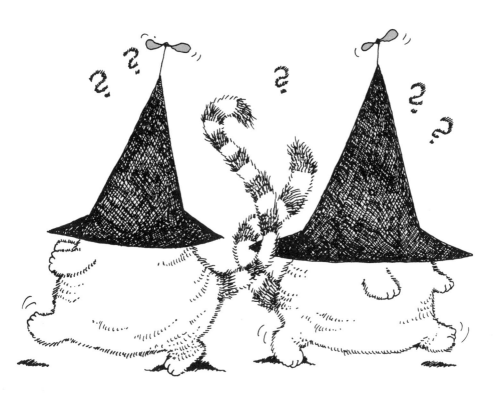

Q: Why were the Halloween cats confused?
A: They didn't know witch way to go.

Q: What kind of coffeepots do cats use?
A: Purr-colators.

Q: Why did the fat cat get even fatter?
A: He ate at every oppor-tuna-ty.

Q: What did the cat pour on his hamburger?
A: Cat-sup.

Q: What are a cat's favorite vegetables?
A: Car-rats and rat-abagas.

Q: What do you call an overweight kitty?
A: A fat cat.

Q: What kind of dance does the Mexico City kitty like to do?

A: The Mexican cat dance.

Q: What do you call a jungle cat who loves to party?

A: A wildcat.

Q: How do mountain lions dance?

A: They lynx their arms together.

Q: What was left when the cat's party was over?
A: Kitty litter.

ABOUT THE ARTIST

JOAN HANSON lives with her husband and two sons in Afton, Minnesota. Her distinctive, deliberately whimsical pen-and-ink drawings have illustrated more than 30 children's books. Ms. Hanson is also an accomplished weaver. A graduate of Carleton College, Hanson enjoys tennis, skiing, sailing, reading, traveling, and walking in the woods surrounding her home.

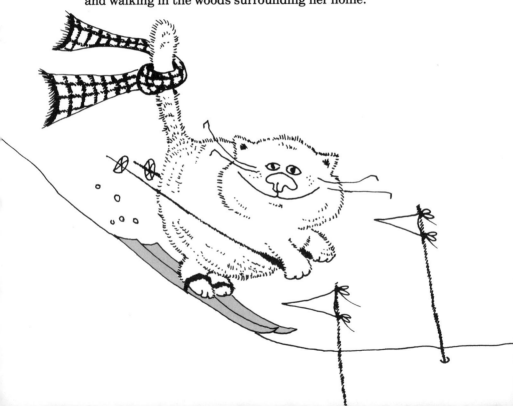

ABOUT THE AUTHORS

SHARON FRIEDMAN lives in Silver Spring, Maryland, with her husband, Stephen, and their two sons, Robbie and Lee. She was a third grade teacher for eight years and is currently the president of her sons' PTA. Sharon enjoys tennis, dancing, and puppetry, and presents puppet shows and puppet-making workshops at area schools.

IRENE SHERE had the expert help of her children, Holly and Brett, when creating and testing these riddles. She enjoys being with children—both as a teacher and as a mother and active school volunteer. Irene spends her free moments drawing, ice skating, and playing with computers. She lives with her husband, Steve, and their children in a glass house surrounded by trees in Silver Spring, Maryland.

Make Me Laugh!

101 ANIMAL JOKES
101 FAMILY JOKES
101 KNOCK-KNOCK JOKES
101 MONSTER JOKES
101 SCHOOL JOKES
101 SPORTS JOKES
CAT'S OUT OF THE BAG!
GO HOG WILD!

GOING BUGGY!
GRIN AND BEAR IT!
IN THE DOGHOUSE!
LET'S CELEBRATE!
OUT TO LUNCH!
SPACE OUT!
STICK OUT YOUR TONGUE!